She Was The Storm

poetry by
Cherie Avritt

for every woman
whose love
could never be contained

-she was the storm

chapter one

woman

you were a flower
blooming
before his very eyes

but he
could not see
your value

i thought
you were perfect
for me

i thought
you would be the one
to capture my heart

but you
were just like the rest

you
betrayed me

you expected perfection
holding me up
to impossible standards

i wish i had known
that was a red flag
but instead
i let you
make me
feel bad
about myself

i was so focused
on the idea
of getting you to love me
that i didn't notice
i was better off
without you

free feelings
the skies open up

i need
to let go of you

i spent too many days
curled up against the window
listening to the rain
incapable of
getting over you

i am tired of giving my
everything
to someone who doesn't notice
my efforts

on some level
i knew you were
just using me
but i didn't want
to admit that
to myself

just because
someone
once hurt you

doesn't mean
that everyone
who comes
after them

also will.

inconsistency
is the first sign
that someone only cares about you
when it's convenient
for them

it's not easy to bury
the remnants
of my love for you

but i must

i must, for my own good.

you
can handle
anything
life
throws
at you.

you felt like home
to me
but now
i am out on the streets
in the cold
without your warmth
without your love

for a second
i almost consider
going back to you

but going through that
all over again
would hurt worse
than the cold outside

you made me feel special
just to get something
from me

you used me
you didn't care
how bad it hurt me

i still think about you
when my hands slip
between my legs
in the middle of the night

even though you hurt me
i can't stop thinking
of you

there is nothing
quite as difficult
as having
to start
all over
again

never give up
you have come too far
and fought too hard
to give up now

it hurts to realize
that no one has ever cared
about me
as much as i
have cared
about them

perhaps i feel too deeply
or get attached too easily

the passion between us
burned hot and fast
it felt like a fairytale

that should've been my first
warning sign;

it was too good to be true
even if i
was unwilling to see that

he may have broken you
but your love
for yourself
can heal you

my long hair waves in the breeze
as i sit on the shore
watching the waves
dash against the rocks

even here, in my happy place
you intrude upon my mind
shoving aside my thoughts
to take your place
at the front
of my mind

i gave you everything
i had
but you didn't care

i have wasted
too many nights
thinking about the way
your love hurt me

she was the sun
hidden for the night
but waiting
to once again
rule over the sky

someone who will love you
for who you truly are
is always worth
the wait

you are special
you are loved
you are appreciated
you are worth the wait

your heart
speaks to mine
in such a beautiful way

x

chapter two

lessons

i have learned many things
in my time
on this earth

the most important
of which
is that
we are all the same
in more ways than we know
and we should love each other
for that reason

—lessons

love never dies.
it is only reborn.

when someone leaves your life
do not blame it on yourself

the universe took them out
of your life
for a reason

never be afraid
to cut toxic people
out of your life
for the sake
of your own happiness

never forget
that you
are
good enough.

like the flick of a light switch
suddenly i saw everything
i saw my own foolishness
in chasing after you
when i knew that it
could never work out

do not forget
to take your own advice

so often we can see
what others need
but are so blind
when it comes to ourselves

do not resent yourself
for how slowly you are healing

it takes time
and you need to remember that.

you can't convince people
to give you
the love you deserve

it may not seem like it
today
but there will come a day
when everything feels okay again

the only one
who can stop you
from living up
to your full
potential

is

you.

what happened
was not your fault
you did nothing wrong

never take for granted
the people in your life
who stand by you
through every struggle

you made me feel
like i could soar
above the clouds
like an eagle

but then
when i stopped being
useful to you
you threw me away
and i fell towards the ground
and with just a few words
you made me feel
like every bone in my body
had been broken

i believe in you
even when
you do not
believe
in yourself

i cannot protect my heart
from the whims of your love
you only love me back
when it suits you

crying
is never weakness

you were always the one
i could lean on
when life felt impossible

but now
you are out of my life
and i have no one
to lean on

one day
you will find
your balance again;

this i promise you.

i hate the way
things ended
between us

i never got
an explanation
i never understood
why you left

you will make it through this
just like you've made it
through everything else
that has come before

let me dress your wounds
and hold you tightly
as you sob in my arms

i will hold you
as long as it takes
until you feel okay
again

do not hurt others
in the same way
you've been hurt before

x

chapter three

hurricane

she was the hurricane
whirling through the landscape
taking no prisoners
taking all the power
for herself

deciding to move on
is the hardest part

you make me feel good
about myself
even when i
cannot find a shred of light
amidst the darkness

never forget
your own
value.

never allow others
to tell you
you aren't good enough

i could get lost
in your words
they brush against my mind
like silk against the hand
soft and luxurious
inviting and loving

you will get through this
just as you
have gotten through
every struggle
that came before

never stop
believing
in yourself

she was an oasis
in the desert
bringing back life
when it seemed to have vanished

stop questioning
your instincts
and start following them

every word of love
and compassion
you utter

makes a difference
in others' lives

i keep rehearsing
what i would say to you
to myself in the mirror

but it's no use;
i know i could never
work up the courage
to tell you
the truth

beware of people
who find it easy
to walk away

i will hold you
tenderly
when the world hurts

she was the light
beaming from behind the mountains
illuminating the lost souls
and bringing comfort to the
broken

loving others
teaches you
to love
yourself

the greater
your current struggle
the greater
the light is
at the end
of the tunnel

your future
is bright
and everything
will turn out
okay

the minutes
i spend with you
keeps me going
through hard hours
of work and pain

my hopes for you
were proven wrong
one too many times

it is okay to admit
to yourself
that you aren't okay.

x

chapter four

storm

she was the storm
a force of nature;
once she had discovered
her true power
suddenly she became
unstoppable

how are you supposed
to follow your heart
when it is broken and bleeding?

i would rather have
a thousand bruises
than feel again
the pain of you
leaving me

never allow anyone
to treat you
as if you
are just another option

don't spend your life
waiting
for an apology
that will never come.

beware those
who only take from you
and never give back

i wanted your love
to fix me
but you only left me
more broken
than i was
in the beginning

the world
piles on top of me
my breathing is constricted
my lungs cry for air

i cannot just forgive you
for what you did
to me

i don't hate you
but i can't just pretend
you never broke me

is this
what love
is
supposed to feel like

or am i
just desperately trying
to justify the way
you treat me
because i'm too afraid
to let go

to live
a life
of positivity
you must surround yourself
with positive people

surround yourself
with positive energy
and cut off those
with toxicity

you are better off
without them

we are only
searching for things
in others
that we wish we had
ourselves

i want to give you
everything
i was never given
throughout my life

find the light
within yourself
and set it free

do not try so hard
to help others
that you forget
your own needs

touch my soul
gently with your hands
smooth out the shards
of my broken heart

don't waste "i love you's"
on people
who don't understand
what that truly means

there will always be
another chance
to not repeat
your mistakes

the greatest joy
is in realizing
that your broken heart
finally doesn't hurt
anymore

this book of poetry is for you.
the broken hearted soul in need
of encouragement. let me remind
you who you truly are. you are
the power of nature, waiting to
take the world by storm.

-Cherie Avritt